THE SOUL OF
Teaching

ENCOURAGEMENT FOR HIGH SCHOOL
TEACHERS AND PRINCIPALS
WHO SOMETIMES

JOHN H___

ILLUSTRATIONS BY MARY HERBIN-HORAN

THE SOUL OF TEACHING
Encouragement for High School Teachers and Principals
Who Sometimes Might Need It
John Horan
with illustrations by Mary Herbin-Horan

Edited by Gregory F. Augustine Pierce
Design and typesetting by Patricia A. Lynch

Copyright © 2020 by John Horan

Published by ACTA Publications, 4848 N. Clark Street, Chicago, IL 60640,
(800) 397-2282, www.actapublications.com

Library of Congress Control Number: 2020943556
ISBN: 978-0-87946-685-5

Printed in the United States of America by Total Printing Systems
Year 35 34 33 32 31 30 29 28 27 26 25 24 23 22 21 20
Printing 20 19 18 17 16 15 14 13 12 11 10 9 8 7 6 5 4 3 2 First

CONTENTS

DEDICATION

To Chris Kelly—visionary, peerless engineer, and tireless advocate for young people who are underserved and underestimated. You are my first and best reader and the constant hope that animates these pages.

INTRODUCTION
THE SEARCH FOR SOUL

There is a love like a small lamp, which goes out when the oil is consumed;
or like a stream, which dries up when it doesn't rain.
But there is a love that is like a mighty spring gushing up out of the earth;
it keeps flowing forever and is inexhaustible.

Isaac of Nineveh

On my first day of 4th grade, my teacher rocked my world. She wrote her name, *Mrs. Rosemary Cantlin*, on the chalk board in the most perfect Palmer Method handwriting I have ever seen. She then finished the final "n" with an enthusiastic flourish.

She then turned to the class and said, "Look at my name. Within it you will find a four-letter word that is a contraction of two words. Who can spot it?" When the nervous titters (mostly among the boys) over the phrase "four-letter word" had died down, we nine-year-olds got down to business. After a flurry of raised hands and bouncing desks, Mrs. Cantlin called on one of us. My first true love in my young life, Kimberly Oswald, raised her hand and shouted: "*Can't*, Ms. Cantlin! *Can not! Can't!*"

"Precisely," said Mrs. Cantlin. "*Can't*. And that is the last time you will use that four-letter word in my class."

Mrs. Cantlin was a teacher whose love was like a mighty spring gushing up out of the earth. Flowing forever. Inexhaustible.

Although our schools may be public or charter, parochial or private, in home or in a big or tiny building, they are all spiritual places. The soul of teaching belongs to no one faith, denomination, or philosophy, but it encompasses all of them. In these days of chasing standardized test metrics, common cores, and budget crises, it is easy to forget that schools are the setting for the life of the spirit. Each school has a soul, and so does each teacher, principal, student, parent, and support staff.

Great schools are acts of love. They come from the deepest core of interactions between students and teachers. But we teachers and principals can run dry. Our lights can be extinguished. The reflections in this little book are reminder notes about how we educators abide in a love that is a mighty spring and how we give and receive that love every day.

Blessed is the influence of one, true loving human soul on another.

George Elliot/Mary Ann Evans

∞

- Like the wind, "soul" is known only by its movement. It lives in the in-between of students and teachers, a school community, and the world.

- "Teaching" is a gerund; a noun married to a verb. It is known only in and through relationships. All of us are always both the teachers and the taught.

- A student is awe-struck by a teacher's observation that she is really, really smart. How did Tierra go so long without being told? Students are a sail, begging for a breeze. Teachers are sailors always tacking into the wind. Soul moves across the waters and propels our students forward to their undiscovered selves. And in so doing, we find our better selves.

- A library full of 9th-grade parents at an orientation blink back tears hoping that the soaring rhetoric of the school's mission will do more than quicken their hearts. They wonder if it will be matched by a day by day intentionality lead by school staff they have yet to come to know and trust. Soul is a wager on promises to be kept by teachers yet unknown.

- An entire school staff surrounds the perimeter of their school. The faculty was a buffer between their students and the madness of a mob. The teachers were awed by their own efficacy. Who knew that their students would come to mean so much to them? The teachers were peace warriors, love's mission incarnate, willing to pay the price. They stood, shoulder to shoulder, heart to heart. Their students never saw such a lesson plan. Soul is the outbreak of outrageous hope.

- The soul of teaching bends time. We have been apprenticed by great teachers. Because we have been well-taught, we want to do for our students what our teachers past did for us. Our history informs our present and we pour out our vital energies in the hope that our students will, in turn, pay this precious DNA forward in a future yet unseen.

- The soul of teaching habituates us to doing good. The daily life of a school presents a million opportunities to do good. We get hooked on spiritual endorphins. We see more, give more, put more resources in play and become finely tuned instruments of grace. When we abide in soul, we cannot help but give ourselves away. Doing good begets good.

- The soul of teaching thrives on making a way out of no way. Teachers tilt at windmills thirsty for an impossible dream. We insist that a student's damaged past need not be prelude to their future. We plant fields for a harvest that we will never see. We insist that in our place, on our watch, love will find a way and our students will grow into their best selves.

- The movement of soul is the language of the metaphor. Wind. Sails. Promises kept. Outrageous hope. DNA. Good begetting good. Finding a way out of no way. The best thing to do is to reflect on our rich experience and share our stories of the in-between.

- Love is the first and most important lesson plan in the soul of teaching. We teachers and principals know that all growth happens in the context of deep relationships between young people and mindful adults. We can only go deep with young people if we stay deep. Staying deep is, at its core, a spiritual enterprise.

PART ONE

WHAT DO YOU SEE?

The eyes are the windows of the Soul.

William Shakespeare

- If one is able, as the old English proverb goes, to look into someone's eyes and see their soul, then what do you see as your students saunter in on a Monday morning? How does that which animates you, your profoundest sense of meaning, shape how and what you see? And how does what you see in your students affirm, critique and enlarge your own soulfulness? And will your students get close enough for you to see their soul?

- As importantly, what do your students see as they look into your eyes? Mercy? Joy? Resilience? Wisdom? Acceptance? A fierce and curious intellect? An unwavering belief? Uncompromising expectation? A safe harbor? A valence between who they long to be and what you will come to mean to them? And will you get close enough so that your students can see your soul?

- What do you see when you look at your classroom? A classroom has a soul. Are there "ins and outs"? Who hides in silence behind hoodies, ear buds or serial snoozing? Is there safety enough for those who risk being smart, different, or special?

- Can your students belong to each other and practice the habit of community? Do they cheer for each other and weep over suffering shared? Classroom soul is a safety net and a launching pad, it is cartilage between rough fractures, a "double-dare you" and a safe space for all of life's tough landings.

- It is said that adolescent cynicism is their idealism spurned. Do your students itch to take on the world, the most important final exam? Do they have a place to stand, truths to speak? Do they rage against justice delayed, experience each other as a force for good, as a remedy for what ails their neighborhood? In Gandhi's words, are they the change they long to be in the world? And can you help them see this power?

HOW TO SAY "HEY"
EVERY MONDAY MORNING

My father once went through 14 hours of surgery to save his right leg. When the surgery was over, he struggled back to consciousness. My mom, at his side through every moment in the ICU, held his face in her hands, caught his eyes, and said, "HEY!"

Say "HEY" every Monday morning, as one greeting a much beloved who has been long asleep.

About a year ago, I misplaced my wedding ring and couldn't find it for two months. When I found it buried in my sock drawer, I said, "HEY!"

Say "HEY" every Monday morning, as one discovering a ring that summons your solemn promise.

Think of your favorite meal in your favorite restaurant with a generous pour of your favorite wine. You are starving. The meal is placed before you and you say, "HEY!"

Say "HEY" every Monday morning, as one anticipating a glorious meal.

When we greet our students every Monday morning, what we believe we are seeing will shape how we say "HEY!"

Here is what we can see IF we look.

- Each student is a Rubik's Cube.
- Each student's brain has more neurons than there are stars in the galaxy.

If we believe we are greeting a young person who longs to be awake,

If we believe we are seeing a ring that summons our solemn promise,

If we believe we are beginning a banquet that will fill our students' hunger for meaning and slake our own thirst for justice,

Well, then, we will give our students quite a greeting: HEY!

OPENING OUR DOORS

Tomorrow, as inevitable as the dawn — unless there is another natural or humanmade crisis — our school doors will swing open.

We are ready to teach our students life readiness and higher order thinking skills.

We are ready to teach our students how to find their inner strength, how to see hope in a darkened world, and how to be change agents for a better day.

We are rested, fired up, and ready to give all we have in service to all our students coming through the doors.

That is how it should be. But that is not all it can be. What if we flipped the script? What if we focused on what our students are about to give *us*?

If we really believe in our students' potential, surely they will bestow on us gifts powerful, sundry, and unpredictable. We are not the only "givers" in this relationship. Real school spirit demands that we stay awake and constantly be attentive to *their* power to gift *us*.

Open the doors.

- Someone will transfuse you with exuberance.
- Someone will awaken in you an empathy so deep and painful that you will cry yourself to sleep.
- Someone will unpack for you the invisible backpack of white privilege.
- Someone will amaze you with their power to escape the gravity of the two dark moons of violence and poverty.
- Someone will draw forth from you reserves of love and hope you never knew you had.
- Someone will catch your heart off guard — and blow it wide open.

What will our students give us? We will find out only when we are truly open to receive it.

And when we do this, we will ineluctably find ourselves closer to the Beloved Community of Teachers to which we aspire. The respect and love we want to see happening in every hallway and every classroom will be happening already. That's because respect isn't a matter of etiquette and manners. It is a matter of soul. And beholding the gifts our students offer us is the truest expression of respect.

So, open the doors and let them in!

BREATHE IN, BREATHE OUT

I once had lunch with a principal from another school. I was about to tear into my meal with all the frenzied speed and lack of manners that is my habit, when she stopped me. She said that before her kindergarten students eat, they take 3 deep breaths and then say, "Thank you, thank you, thank you." She asked that we do the same. So, I took three deep breaths and quietly said, "Thank you, thank you, thank you."

It was nice. It slowed me down from my usual breakneck speed. It centered me in the here and now. And the "thank you's" were wonderful. They were open-ended. I could have been thanking the farmers who grew the food, the school chef who prepared it, or my friend for sharing it.

This is how we teachers and principals need to start each day: Breathing out and breathing in, trying to slow down from the rush of making lesson plans, taking meetings, copying handouts, and arranging seating charts. We need to center ourselves in the great work we are called to do. We are all working on a mystery. It helps when that mystery comes from our deep heart's core.

And we should say thank you: to our loved ones who keep us whole, to our colleagues who lift us up, to all the students who have smartened us up and will continue to do so again. We are a lucky bunch, to do such important work. I am so glad we get to do this together.

So, before you jump into the delicious meal that is teaching:

> Breathe in, breathe out,
> Breathe in, breathe out,
> Breathe in, breathe out,
> Say thank you, thank you, thank you.

WHAT GOT YOU OUT OF BED
THIS MORNING?

It is a tough morning, that first day back from a wonderful holiday vacation that seemed to linger on and on.

It may be tough to leave our family after having spent so much quality time with them. (As the son of a fellow faculty member remarked when she headed back to school recently, "Mom, it's been great to be with you. See you again in May!")

It is tough to leave afternoon naps, TV binge watching, catching up with friends, reading for pleasure (Whaaa?), and waking up every morning knowing that the day is entirely yours (or at least it is not dominated by students and parents and principals)!

So this is what we need to remember as we head back to school, whether it is after a weekend or a summer or a year:

- Teaching is a chance for us to do good that matters.

- Teaching, although it sometimes depletes our energy and devours our time, also deepens our humanity.
- Teaching is a chance to disrupt our world's increasing tolerance for violence in thought, word, and deed.
- Teaching is a chance to help our students experience their potential and take the risks necessary to be full grown.
- Teaching is a chance for us to love and be loved back by surprising, garrulous, and abundant kids.
- Teaching is a chance to counter the terrible causality of generational poverty, kid by kid, family by family, block by block.
- Teaching is a chance to work with other teachers and administrators as we strive to give our students the great school they deserve and build the school we all long to be.

Teaching is tough work and we have no illusions about what it will demand of us. But if you, like me, were blessed by the abundance of our friends and family, it is once again time to pay that abundance forward.

KID CAPTURED BY A FIRE HYDRANT

I was running laps in Douglas Park in Chicago when I came across a metaphor.

A young mom dressed in a nurse's aid's uniform was pushing a beat-up stroller carrying a squalling infant. Mom rolled by on wobbly wheels.

Twenty-five feet behind her another child, maybe 3-4 years old, was in a fix. He had somehow pulled the front of his sweatshirt up and over a fire hydrant. His futile struggles to free himself only bound him more hopelessly. Terror was settling in. His wail rose like a police siren as the distance between his mom and him grew.

And, what did I do? Well, heck, I'm a teacher. I help kids free themselves from the things that bind. So, I did it again. I helped the little boy get his sweatshirt up and over the fire hydrant. He was off like a shot, ready to investigate Douglas Park, swirling leaves, loose soccer balls, the paletas cart, and finally the outstretched arms of his waiting mother.

Trying to get out of bed on a Monday morning can sometimes make us teachers feel like we are dragging a fire hydrant behind us. We have no illusions about how hard we will work, the challenges we will face, and the energy required to sustain a great school. But the call to something greater lifts us up. We are called to help kids of all ages free themselves from the things that bind. It is a long list, and we only know the half of it. It will require our best energy and robust hope. But the joy of witnessing a young person, unbound, interrogating the universe, makes it all worth it.

Have a great week doing great school. And if you see a colleague hung up on a fire hydrant, slow your run and help her/him get free.

HEATING UP THE FILAMENT

My wife and I are using these new light bulbs. They use less energy and supposedly will shine well past my retirement. They are very expensive (we had to refinance our house in order to buy a pack of six), but they have a most agreeable feature. When you turn on the bulb, they light gradually, starting with a barely visible, comfortable hobbit-hole glow, which soon works its way to full light. It is a matter of filament, the thread-like conductor that has to be heated to incandescence.

I don't know about you, but after a few-days break from school, it takes my filament a little time to heat up. We teachers and principals go back at this demanding work with no illusions about how much will be required of us. The work is simultaneously exhilarating and exhausting. We aim not to just "get through" a quarter or semester or year, but we want to heat ourselves to incandescence. We are after the high ground of teaching kids: the lighting of fires that will burn a lifetime. But it will usually take us a bit to heat up:

- We heat up because our school and our mission is the right thing for these muddled times, an antidote to poverty, an outbreak of justice.

- We heat up because we get to work with our colleagues–smart, resilient, resourceful, deep souled, bodacious do-gooders.
- We heat up because of our kids, and the opportunity to challenge, celebrate, and just plain love them. And be challenged, celebrated, and loved back by them in return.

So goodbye afternoon naps. So long to waking up after 8 am. Arrevadercie to staying up way late and goofing around. It is back to incandescence. I hear coffee helps.

NEWSPAPER GUY

There is this guy who sells newspapers every morning. Drive through the intersection of Sacramento and Harrison and you will see him there, as consistent as gravity. He stands on a traffic island selling the *Sun Times*, the *Tribune*, and the *Defender* to northbound and southbound traffic on Sacramento. It is a death-defying occupation…and location.

In the summer, he also sells cold water and fruit. As the Christmas tide rushed in this past December, he donned a Santa's hat. He wears a bright orange vest. There is no missing him. My sense is that people look for him every morning. I know I do. And his consistent presence through the skin-freezing arctic winds of January and the hellish heat of August is strangely comforting. Each day, come hell or high water, Juan is there. As the Rock of Gibraltar is to the Mediterranean Sea, the newspaper guy is to the river of working stiffs flowing down Sacramento Boulevard in Chicago, Illinois.

Juan, the newspaper guy, reminds me of every teacher. We show up every day. We are gravity in a topsy-turvy, capricious, and sometimes cruel universe. We sell good news in a death-defying location. There is no missing us. And our kids look for us, every day, taking comfort in our resilient, consistent, stubbornly hopeful, brain-healing, potential-lighting kind of way.

And here they come. Our students. They will roll into school--a beautiful, raucous, outrageous river. They will dance on our last nerves. They will break our hearts. But mostly they will rise like a Phoenix. What a calling we teachers have! What a special group of high-performing, inexhaustibly hopeful, seriously tough, dedicated adults we are! How did we get so lucky to land this job?

So, here's to the newspaper guy in all of us. Let's DELIVER that good news we are selling. Remember, it is a mere 87 school days until our next semester break.

STRETCHING OUT

You may not know this, but schools often have one of the busiest indoor tracks in the city. It starts at the library doors and finishes at the gym. On any given day after school, you will witness sprinting, hurdling, baton handling, high-jumping, and shot-putting. Coach is still trying to figure out how to teach javelin-tossing. (1st floor English and Spanish teachers beware!)

My favorite part of track practice is the warm-ups. Before the hard, sweaty business of running begins, the athletes must stretch out. They do this in a wide variety of ways. Coach has them take exaggerated, lunging giant steps — straight out of Monty Python's Ministry of Silly Walks. Next, the runners stick out their arms in front at shoulder length and kick each leg up and out, touching toe to palm over and over again for the length of the hall. What proceeds next is a series of impossible bends and tendon stretches that would put most of us teachers and administrators in a body cast.

Only then do the students begin to run.

It seems to me that we teachers must do some stretching out of our own before we begin our daily teaching runs. For example, we cannot just jump right into Period 1 without stretching out first, without re-establishing the "WHY?"

behind all our work, the context from which all our efforts issue forth. Here are two stretches you can do, often in seconds, just before you know what hits the you know what. Just take a moment and remember:

- Everything we do should stretch the possibility for peace. We should help our kids experience, long for, and teach the concept of a Beloved Community, moving them from victimhood to victory, from pathology to potential, from by-standers to up-standers.
- Everything we do should stretch to create more opportunities to move all our students to a radically different life for themselves and their children. Talent is more evenly distributed than opportunity. Our job is to put our thumbs on the opportunity scale.

So, take a deep breath before Period 1, teachers and principals. Stretch out. Remember why we are here. Re-establish the context from which all your efforts will flow. Today will be a sprint. The hurdles are high, the shotput is heavy, and the marathon is long. But what a race it will be, and best of all we get to do it together.

RABID

She blew in the school's entrance with the Polar Vortex at her back. Her coat, more suited for mid-May than the depths of January, was wrapped tightly around her stick-thin frame. Her bookbag provided ballast, her boots were more fashion statement than protection, and her mismatched gloves were entirely without fingertips.

And strangely enough, she carried a kitchen broom — a broom with worn, angled plastic bristles held in place by a plastic brush-cap connected to a scuffed shaft and neon orange handle. No more than a $4.99 purchase at the local thrift store.

It was early, easily 45 minutes before the first bell. When she stopped shivering and stamping her feet, I asked why she carried the broom with her. "The dogs" she said. "There's a pack of rabid dogs in the park."

(Note: When I drive to school in a cozy car every morning, I never notice a pack of rabid dogs patrolling the adjacent park. Thus does material abundance limit our vision.)

Tyra continued. "They are really skinny dogs and looking for food. And they come running at me when I cut through the park. They nearly bit me yesterday. I think they are crazy rabid. So today I have the broom. I swung it at them and they ran away."

Polar Vortex, rabid dogs, a broom — as amazing as these details were, it was equally amazing that Tyra, habitually late, had come to school so early, especially on a morning so cold.

"It's Mr. T," she proudly informed me. "He is tutoring me. He says I am good in math."

"Good" was not an adjective usually used to describe Tyra. But Mr. T had said she was good in math, that she had a talent, that he would help her get ahead of everyone if she came in early. Both teacher and student were willing to walk the extra mile.

Mr. T had had a sixth sense, as all great teachers do, for students who are what I call "hope deprived." It was not hard to see that Tyra came to school early as much for Mr. T's loving regard as she did for his polynomials.

I told her I would store her broom in my office. I wanted to be close to this totem of teacher-student power.

Sure enough, Tyra's grades rose with the outside temperature. The "A" she received in math pulled up her other grades, and for the first time in her life she landed on the honor roll and not the suspension list.

I still have her broom in my office, a graduation gift from Tyra, a daily reminder that a teacher's honest praise melts the polar vortex of the most hope-deprived student's heart. And that teacher's belief in their students' potential sweeps them off their feet and makes them rabid for a new horizon.

WE HAVE NO IDEA

Jerome knew right away that the college campus in Mississippi was not safe. The two security guards were over 60 years old and drove golf carts around campus that were at least as old as them. They rarely left their guard house. The joke was that they had futons on the floor. Whenever the security guards attempted to impose order, everyone laughed.

Shots were fired at the first off-campus party of the year. Fifty rounds. No joke. It was a miracle no one was injured. Town kids battled the college kids for control of an outside basketball court. The townies always appeared around dusk and were everywhere. There were no gates to separate the town from the college. They hovered around the residence halls, looking for confrontations.

The townies knew that Jerome was from Chicago. Fighting him was irresistible, a chance to show the Chi-raq kid what tough really was. Jerome knew he was living an irony. He had left Chicago because he always had to watch his back, only to go hundreds of miles to a rural college where he always had to watch his back. Going back to Chicago was impossible for Jerome, however. He was determined (partly because of my encouragement) to get a college degree, and Mississippi was where he had the best chance to get one. Staying in Mississippi, however, was dangerously risky. What was a sharp black college freshman to do?

Jerome hunkered down. He cautiously made his way to and from classes and the cafeteria. He rarely went out after dinner and never (I mean never) ventured off campus. The basketball court was a no-fly zone. He stayed in his room most of the time. The weekends were the worst, because most of the students took off. But he couldn't afford to.

I was puzzled when Jerome asked me for books. Books? Don't you have all your classroom books? No, these were different, he explained. He needed to read some interesting books to pass the time. Not stuff he had to read. Stuff he wanted to read. And he had come back to his old high school teacher to ask for a list.

No scary books, he insisted. No science fiction, he didn't like aliens. No books about Michael Jordan, he had read them all. None of that hobbit stuff either. No detective books — he knew the streets too well to believe most of those. "Interesting books," Mr. Horan. "Interesting books, like the ones you used to recommend to us in high school.

So Jerome and I brainstormed and Amazoned this list back in 2020:

- *Between the World and Me* — by poet and social critic Ta-Nehisi Coates
- *Miracle at Santa Anna* — a great war book and film by Spike Lee
- *The Hate You Give* — by Angie Thomas and another major film

With these and other books he came up with himself, Jerome survived his freshman year. He read so he wouldn't be killed. Not exactly the best educational strategy in the world, but one begins where one can.

We teachers have no idea some of the things our our students must face after they leave us. Our job is to prepare them as well as we can. If we are really, really lucky, they come back and ask us for more help.

ENGINEER EYES

The head engineer at the high school burst into my office, breathless with outrage. "YOUR KIDS HAVE GRAFFITIED THE WALLS OF AN ENTIRE CLASSROOM. NEVER SAW ANYTHING SO BAD IN MY LIFE. IT IS AWFUL!" He went on to say that inspectors were coming to examine the building and the damage to this classroom was outrageous and the school would have to pay for the clean-up right away. He stormed off in a cloud of Lysol and righteous indignation.

I trudged upstairs to inspect the damage, bracing myself for words and images that would make a truck driver blush.

Sure enough, the walls were covered with words and images. But this was not X-rated stuff. The art teacher explained that the charcoal sketches were the prep work for a full-classroom mural she wanted the students to produce. There were silhouettes of bodies in motion and inspirational quotes about creativity. Upon completion, our students would be surrounded by the vibrant and passionate work of their hands, hearts, and eyes.

You can't really blame the engineer. For a custodian, every Sharpie is the enemy of a clean, cinder-block wall. But we teachers and principals can question the ways our own perspectives can be highly negatively conditioned. When it comes to kids, too many of us have cataracts:

- When we look at our young people, we must strive to see their powerful potential and not the potential pathology that too many assume.
- When we look at the corrosive effects of poverty, we must not see an excuse for under-achievement but an asset for college resilience.
- When we see our incoming freshmen, we must see college graduates, diploma in hands, no one left behind, all moving on to a life rich with possibilities.

At the end of the day, what separates an average school from a great school is the way each sees their kids. The good ones see artists and idealists, potential and power, they see students thirsty for peace and hungry for healthy community, students who want to achieve in school and go on to do great things. Take another look. See through the graffiti. It is the best cataract treatment you will ever find.

JUKING AT CLUB EUROPEAN

A man was passing out postcard invitations at dismissal. He was at the entrance of the school putting these mini advertisements into the hands of our female students. He seemed to favor our youngest girls.

The postcard invited our young women to the "Up and Down Juke Jam" at "Club European" (apparently located behind the Marathon gas station) that coming Saturday night. I asked the man to get out and escorted him off the school property eight times. He just kept coming, displaying all the persistence and dead-eyed personality of a pit bull (and this is giving pit bulls a bad rap). Many of the man's postcard invites ended up on the sidewalk, but not all.

How does a teacher or principal (or parent for that matter) respond to such trolling? I thought of dressing up in lederhosen and crashing the "party," but this would be at best a temporary distraction and at worst get me a black eye or a night at Cook County Jail. The fact of the matter is that our young charges are not only exposed to the nastiness of the world, but that the nastiness stalks them.

And what should a great school do to help? We can't protect kids from the encroachments of "Club European," but we can launch our kids into the abundance of the world. Summer internships are a good example. When six weeks at Andover College or Google headquarters or the Mayor's office is compared to a night at "Club European," our students can make some informed choices.

When one of our classes or courses fires up the intellectual curiosity and confidence of our students, maybe then the sad trivializing of the Juke Jam becomes more apparent to our students. A great school that launches kids into abundance is no guarantee, but it helps. And it is waaaaay better than seeing me in my lederhosen.

RELENTLESS

Relentless is my new favorite word for teacher. It is based on the Latin word *lentore*, which means "There is no bend here!" Here is what I mean:

- When our students complain to us that "You EXPECT too much of us," we should respond, "Thank You for Noticing." No Bend!
- When our students try the tactics of dis-engagement, vociferous complaining, or just plan giving up, we should look for new and craftier ways to challenge them. No Bend!
- When our students try and slip back to the code of the streets, we should insist on the higher ground of peace-making. No Bend!
- When we come up against the million-and-one terrible manifestations of poverty, we will be relentless in our hope. No Bend!

We will be relentless because our students are full of potential and beauty. We will be relentless because they are intellectually powerful but sometimes fragile. We will be relentless because their voices matter. We will be relentless because they are thirsty for a better world. We will be relentless because they must be relentless. It is that kind of world.

Now go surround some hapless freshman and, in unison, ask that he tuck in his shirt and straighten his tie. And then work your way down the hallway. Relentless. No Bend!

ARE YOU PROUD OF ME?

Tineshia is a world class obfuscator. She has earned this distinction the hard way. She and her mom have been living in a homeless shelter for the past three years. Tineshia is good at fending off questions and delaying appointments. Evasion is her first instinct. My guess is that there are lots of social workers in her life sticking their noses in her business. Such is the price a young person pays for living in a shelter. So Tineshia has developed an almost involuntary, well-practiced defense system:

> Teacher — "Tineshia, let's go to this job fair on Friday."
> Tineshia— "I already have a job."
> Teacher — "Really! That's great. Where is it?"
> Tineshia— "Downtown."
> Teacher — "Where?"
> Tineshia — "I don't know the building's name."
> Teacher — "What is the job?"
> Tineshia — "They haven't told me yet."

A day later she will forget that this conversation ever happened.

At times, Tineshia's avoidance takes the form of a pending doctor's appointment. At other times, she will lash out in anger at some imagined insult: *"I will come and talk to you as soon as you stop acting like a child!"* The background on Tineshia's texts is green. There are miles and miles of her green texts on my phone, a tsunami of excuses, dodges, and feints. Who knows what causes her to self-protect in such a fashion?

But then, there she is: "Are you proud of me?" A simple green text sent after she secured an appointment to be interviewed for a real job.

"Are you proud of me?" If texts could whisper, this would be a whisper.

It was a real interview…for a real job…at a real place…for a real salary. It was a huge break-through for Tineshia. Amid all the evasions and false starts comes this real thing. The real Tineshia wants to know if we are proud of her.

I am always amazed at how our students respond to our honest pride in them. They are doing things that require profound courage: going downtown for an interview, attending a college nine hours away from friends and families, finding their new "self" away from the hood. We teachers can forget how huge these baby steps are. The truth is that there are so many things we can be proud of. We should never miss a chance to answer their question, "Are you proud of me?" Like any one of us, they are longing to be told.

ONE TRUE THING

Edmund Husserl was an early 20th-century philosopher whose big idea was Phenomenology. His claim was that if we deeply reflect on one particular experience, that specific reflection would yield a consciousness of the very contours of being. It would be "ontological," which is philosopher-talk for "one true thing."

Take an experience you have had in teaching — one you regard as the best, most authentic moment you have had with students. Now, reflect on it. Go deep. What is the essential, no-can-do-without truest thing that emerges? What is the one true thing that presents itself, the one true thing that anchors all else?

I'll give you an example from my own teaching. I taught Public Speaking for over eight years. One semester, I had a particularly tough bunch of 26 seniors. It was uphill most of the way, but the kids and I stuck it out as best we could and tried to get it right.

The final speeches of the semester came and, OMG, the talks were good. Very good. All of them! Many of the students brought all the rhetorical skills I had tried to teach together in speeches that were deep and meaningful. Feedback was rich and insightful. Many of them tried new topics and approaches. Some even went back to work on speeches that in light of their classmates' success did not quite hit the high bar their peers had established. Their second try was much improved over their first in every case.

These are the "one true things" that I take away from this experience:

- Real achievement matters to kids.
- Real achievement happens in robust community, over time.
- When real achievement happens, everyone recognizes it happened.
- Once you have experienced real achievement, you hunger for more. It has a life-time resonance. It has the ability to heal.

These are now rock-solid truths for me. But mine is just one voice. As you reflect on your own experience of an authentic teaching experience, what emerges? What is the "one true thing," for you — the essential insight that anchors all else for you about teaching?

My hunch is that there is a grand convergence among us teachers. What anchors you, anchors me, anchors all of us. This is the stuff that establishes a true longitude and latitude that will contextualize budget crunches and crunching data, KPI's and NCLB requirements, kid drama, teacher fatigue, twists and turns, our highs and our lows.

And one last thing about phenomenological analysis. It is supposed to reveal the contours of being. When we uncover the really real in our reflections, we learn not just about classroom or school. We learn about the way all things are. Here's to potential actualized, to robust community, to hunger for the higher ground, to healing for all.

TRANSFIGURATION

"Jesus went up to the mountaintop, and there he was transfigured in front of his disciples."

When it comes to mountaintops, it is all about the view. From a mountain top, we can see the *connections* of things. It is not that we see more, but that we see more deeply. We see into the miracle, the miracle that was always there but was hidden by our shallow perspective. Until now. Things (and people) are transfigured.

We teachers see transfigurations all the time. Sometimes when we look at our students, we see them, as if all of a sudden. In spite of the shallow perspectives imposed by the daily struggles of homework, assessments, student squabbles, and contests of will, sometimes we see the miracles happen right before our eyes. We see our students for all their beauty and potential. We see them as God does. And it blows our mind.

Getting to the mountaintop is hard. The pitch is severe. The ground gives way beneath our feet. Our breath comes raspy, rapid, and shallow. Our energy flags and our spirit drains. And sometimes the big view, the mountain top view, is fogged in: unclear, dangerous, even cold.

In order to see the transfiguration, we have to survive the tyranny of our schedules. We have to avoid getting bogged down by too much TV, food, booze, triviality, depression, loss of love, loss of heart, the scourge of injustice, the sheer scale of suffering in the world. It is too much for one solitary climber.

Mountains teach us we cannot climb alone. We need to bring others, partners to share the trail. In teaching we call that a "faculty." Faculties help us trust in our bigger view, our belief in the Beloved Community of Teaching, in which God is well pleased.

When it comes to transfiguration, it is all about the view. Eat transfiguration moments like the daily bread they are. Pray into and through your challenges. See with and through the eyes of your colleagues. It is what transfiguration is all about.

IN ACTUS PARENTIS

When it comes to a mother's love, we are always bystanders, small moons privileged to orbit around a powerful sun, mere acolytes in service to a Queen's royal intentions.

Dashoney's mom smiled from the second-floor window. Her daughter was moving back to college for her sophomore year. No longer a rookie at this moving thing, Dashoney had boxed, binned, and bagged her belongings. Easily six times her body weight, Dashoney's possessions filled the van and reflected a sophomore's knowledge of the essentials — fridge, mirror, matching comforter and pillows, clothes for all seasons, shower slippers, and microwave.

Dashoney's mom beamed at her daughter's efficiency and delighted in her quiet courage. My Rav4 was gassed up and ready to go, but it was clear that her mother's love powered all Dashoney's forward motion.

First came the tearful kisses from her siblings — mindful, even in these early years, of how high the bar had been set for them. Mom gave the packed van a last inspection and took in the full wonder of her daughter. A simple, "I love you," a long embrace, and promises to call later that evening were exchanged.

Then mom thanked me for helping — with the packing, with driving her daughter back to college, for my teaching and my support. Gratitude was surely called for, but it was me who owed her the thanks for this bountiful experience. How did I get so blessed, I thought, to be part of such profound, empowering love? I hugged mom back, but a genuflection would have been the more appropriate gesture. A mother's love is a holy blessing.

We teachers are often called to serve our students in ways a parent might. *In Actus Parentis* it is called in Latin. But teachers and principals are only emissaries of the parents' love. It is yet another act of faith parents must make — trusting us to act in their name and in their stead.

We should never tire of acknowledging and thanking parents for giving us this singular privilege.

PART TWO

WHAT BEST AWAKENS YOU TO LOVE?

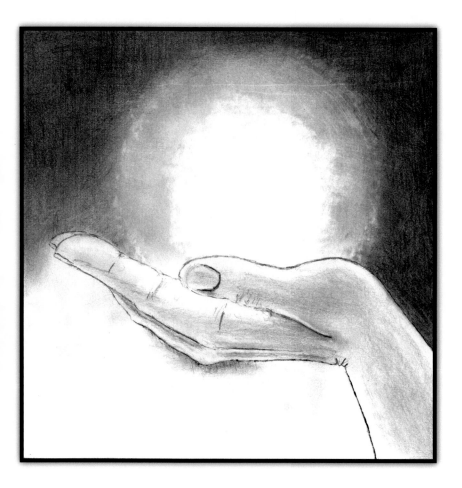

There are only two ways
to live your life.
One is as though nothing is a miracle.
The other is as though everything
is a miracle.

Albert Einstein

- T.S. Eliot says that we are experience rich and meaning poor. This is especially true of teachers. There are all together too many students laying claim to our time and energy. And each student, on any given day, can seem like an entirely different person than the one they were the day or even the hour before.

- Adding to this mighty confusion, is the passage of time. School time is schizophrenic. A day can barrel along at breakneck speed, while some moments move so slowly it is as if they are set in amber. We meet ourselves coming to and going from the parking lot in an exhausted haze. We are sated with experiences but often too short on understanding what our experience means.

- But each day, something happens. Each day there is an interaction, an encounter, a situation, the briefest inclination that stays with us. It is stubborn. It has a certain resonance. A sounding. A hint of a mighty spring. It begs for a diary, for some way in which its meaning can be plumbed before the next mad rush begins.

- It is these special moments that are our daily bread. They are meant to sustain and deepen us, to confirm our deep heart's core or critique how we have lost our most important orientation. They are meant to awaken us to love, the love that is a mighty inexhaustible spring we cannot do without. These everyday revelations, no matter how insignificant they may seem will help us. They are us, talking to us. They are the language of the soul.

BEING CALLED BY NAME

Two years ago, on an early September morning, I spent 2 hours and 20 minutes running 13 miles in the rain. While huffing along I noticed that some smart runners had attached their first name to their Half Marathon t-shirts. This enabled the substantial crowd to shout out encouragement to that person individually rather than with the anonymous encouragement most of the 14,000 runners were getting.

At the 10-mile mark I spied my beautiful bride standing in the rain with a colorful, streaking sign, shouting encouragement to her favorite pre-senior citizen. It was better than Gatorade laced with Advil, better than the theme from Rocky, better than a taxi ride to the finish line.

This is what I learned on that marathon about encouragement in general:

- Anonymous encouragement is good. It beats a stick in the eye.
- Encouragement by name is better. It is always great to hear your name being cheered, even by total strangers.
- But encouragement from one who knows and loves you. Now, that is the best.

And of course, this is also true about teaching. Do we reward our students anonymously — shouting out faceless, generic encouragement as they pass by in a rush? Do we know them by name only? That helps some during a long year's run, but nominal encouragement has a limited shelf time. Or do we know them well — deep down, individually, from their ACT score to their deep heart's core, with a fair measure of love mixed in?

This last one is the best fuel for wobbly legs and a finish line still a distance away.

ENDORPHINS

We have all experienced this after a good workout: that blanket of well-being, the simple glow of our body's ease. Our worries find perspective and our thoughts attain a singular clarity.

Endorphins are the brain's positive reinforcer of our body's labor, that natural chemical after-workout treat. No sooner are we done with our first taste of endorphins than we look forward to the next endorphin reward. Thus do two-miler runners become marathoners.

As physical endorphins are with the body, so too are spiritual endorphins with the spirit. They kick in with us teachers when we:

- celebrate a student's real achievement,
- coach students to and through a new sense of their unique possibility,
- ask a young person the right question at the right time in the right way,
- enable a student to share the burden of an untold sorrow,
- really notice a student and our humanity engages with his or hers or theirs.

We teachers fundamentally change when we are no longer satisfied with the trivial. Spiritual endorphins are our soul's reinforcement of living love's intention. Doing good does us good. Love comes under our roof. Our vocation to teach is affirmed and our hearts become more open to what love requires. There is no going back.

Spiritual endorphins help push us through the fatigue that teaching inevitably brings. They help us run the extra mile and critique our half-efforts. They are balms to the wounds of pessimism and its ugly sister, cynicism. Spiritual endorphins attenuate our self-centeredness. They lift us from the prison of the same-old-same-old and make us thirsty for the next opportunity to love.

The feeling is an inoculation, helping us, for example, to refuse to be suckered into a fight with a student's practiced oppositional defenses and see the real child longing for a better way.

Make no mistake. Unlike physical endorphins, spiritual endorphins are not meant just to make us feel good. They are meant to help us do good, incarnating God's grace so our students can see and feel and taste what love is. They are meant to addict us to the ways of intentional love. They are our deepest heart's lesson plan.

Welcome your soul's release of spiritual endorphins. Get addicted. You are not meant to be a two-miler teacher. You are a marathoner! You are not meant to be a trickle of grace. You are meant to be a marathon of grace.

PISAQUITA

My Italian grandmother had this strange greeting for each of her 26 grandchildren. She called it *"pisaquita."* (I have no idea about this spelling.)

When we walked in her front door, she would pinch our cheeks, stretch out our lips, and then plant an industrial sized kiss on us. She did this every time we came in through her door. She especially loved doing this when her grandchildren were teenagers and "too cool" for *pisaquita*.

My grandmother did this because she was "crazy." She was crazy in love with her grandchildren. *Pisaquita* signaled that her doorway was the entrance into surprising, funny, abundant love, and that her home was a rainbow place in a grimy world.

At one high school campus, the principal and CFO annually played a game of running bases with the entire student body. They eventually tagged out every student. At the same time, wearing what can only be described as a squid's head hat and Incredible Hulk gloves, the dean of students fist-bumped every student as they made an out. The kids *always* cracked up when they were finally tagged. Their mean mug masks (an adaptive technique used to navigate a sometimes grimy world) just melted away, and they became wide awake.

The doorway to our schools should be an entrance into surprising, funny, abundant love. We teachers have a long tradition of greeting kids in *pisaquita* sorts of ways. Faculty members stage double-dutch jump roping competitions. The science department chairs play Broadway show tunes before the start of class. The dean of discipline has led line dancing in the school lobby. (This is pure *pisaquita*.) Not only should teachers **not** rely on metal detectors. *We should be greeting our kids with crazy love.*

At our high school, volunteers from a nearby church greet students back to school each year. They use smurf balls, pom pons, whistles, cowbells, and assorted merry making devices. Crazy love.

Our church greeters are experts in staging a surprising, funny creative way to say "Hello!" How about you? Do you have any *pisaquita* ideas? These greetings must be capable of melting mean mugs and helping kids become wide awake. It has to be pure *pisaquita*. Nothing less will do, right Grandma?

A MATCH-MAKER UNIVERSE

At some point we teachers must decide for ourselves what kind of universe we have (or want).

Astrophysicists and mystics have a certain view. So do generals and geneticists. And optimists and pessimists. And…you get the idea.

My experience as a high school teacher and leader has led me to choose to believe in a "Match-Maker Universe." Just as surely as two hydrogen atoms match up with one oxygen atom to form water, so too does a school's mission match up with hearts that are hungry for hope. We are all — teachers, parents, and principals — waiting to be married to a noble purpose. Sometimes the universe gives us a nudge. Like a match-maker!

There is nothing accidental about students, families, staff, supporters, volunteers, and surrounding community sharing so much space, time, and work as that of a school. We all share the same valance. Then, like a set of curtains, we are drawn together. Our combined power becomes greater than the sum of our parts and stronger than the forces which threaten to tear us asunder. Here's how we do it:

- by forming a peaceful community of robust learning,
- by preparing our students to break the gravity of poverty through education and activism,
- by helping students name and then overcome the thousand-and-one obstacles placed in their way.

This is what a matchmaker universe looks like. It tests all of us individually but then it marries us together, which is one of the most sublime matches ever made.

Giving thanks is being mindful that we have been matched. There is nothing accidental about a soulful school. The universe has nudged us all towards one another — students, faculty, families, supporters and volunteers alike, all of us bound together by our mission, by our common purpose to do uncommon good in this time and place.

So grateful to be by your side!

HOPE

Did you ever notice how often our prayers and fairy tales end with nearly the same words:

- …lived happily ever after.
- …would last forever and ever,
- …how it was, is now and ever shall be.

This convergence of happy endings is no coincidence. Both prayer and fairy tales are wagers based on hope. Especially in a downside-up universe — here the innocent suffer and justice is delayed, and the rich and/or the violent bear things away--prayer and fairy tales must end with hope.

Let me be clear about hope. Real hope has nothing to do with the fragile outcomes of repeated wishes. Real hope is the belief that no matter what happens the process or journey itself will be replete with meaning. Having hope means that — even if our journey ends badly, or sadly, or even tragically--all the coping, caring, depending, loving, and letting go — will be abundantly rich. We will experience and digest profound truths we otherwise would never have seen. Hope is the belief that love will have the final say. Here is how poet, playwright, and the former president of the Czech Republic, Vaclav Havel, said it: "Hope is definitely not the same thing as optimism. It is not the conviction that something will turn out well, but the certainty that something makes sense, regardless of how it turns out."

Teachers bet on hope every day. We believe that our efforts will make a difference, even if we may never observe those results. Even if all current evidence points in exactly the opposite direction, we have at it, day in and day out, because "you never know." Love takes its own sweet time, and it *will* have the final say.

And, truth be told, being hopeful changes us:

- Hope activates providence.
- Hope deepens our humanity.
- Hope defies the strictures of time and space.

I give thanks because you and all our students — past, present, and to come — have taught me the invaluable truth that prayers and fairy tales all end the same way.

METTLE DETECTORS

Imagine going to a friend's home for dinner and being stopped at the threshold; at which point you are immediately patted down and asked to take off your belt or empty your purse. Then you are wanded (think electronic surveillance wand and not fairy tale wand). If an alert is triggered (think sound of a strangling duck) you must repeat the same process all over again, this time minus your cell phone, jewelry, change, shoes, wallet, rings, car keys, and any other remotely metallic object.

Only then, would you be allowed to enter the home. Some welcome. It would be more like entering a penal institution than preparing for a great dinner with those you love. Enjoy that dinner!

What happens at our school thresholds is like an overture to a symphony; a quick sampling of the most prized themes that will be played over and over again inside. We tell our students what we really think of them when they enter our schools. Is it a prison prep pat down, or a college/career prep hello, or something in between?

There are thoughtful people on both sides of the school metal detector debate. But there is little doubt what the answer will be for schools who serve under-resourced brown or black kids. Not only are these schools under-resourced, they are underestimated. What if we did a homonym switch: swapping *metal* detectors for *mettle* detectors? How would this change our practice?

Mettle means vigor, stamina, and strength of spirit. Poor kids have these qualities in abundance, although we don't give them credit nearly enough: At 15 years of age, many of them have withstood more heartbreak and deprivation than we will experience in a lifetime. Who knows what burdens they carry day in and day out? They have stamina.

Vigor does not only belong to cheerleaders. The act of will required to escape the daily, terrible gravity that poverty imposes is nothing short of world-class. The very act of our students crossing our thresholds displays a vigor that, however muted, is nevertheless profoundly hopeful and life-affirming.

The strength of spirit displayed by our students when they become the first from their family to go to college is remarkable. Consistently summoning the strength to be one of the few people of color attending a predominantly white institution is a strength few of us possess. For the first time in their lives, our minority students will be the only black face in a classroom, on the quad, or in the dorm. They will be objects of curiosity, condescension, and often racism. In classroom discussions they will be asked to be the "spokesperson" for their entire race. This strength of spirit is rarely found among young people, even in our churches, mosques and synagogues.

What are our school thresholds like? What messages are we sending at the thresholds of our school, classrooms, cafeteria, library, and offices? Are students celebrated for their mettle and vigor, or are they profiled for some imagined/potential pathology? Each day, are they celebrated for their strength of spirit?

Although there is an honest disagreement about school metal detectors, in my opinion there can be none when it comes to school mettle detectors.

A RED VINES SORT OF PLACE

Red Vines are the poor man's (and poor woman's) Twizzlers. Red Vines come in a transparent tub, 250 of them in all, weighing in at 4 pounds. They usually cost about $9, but if you watch the prices, you can nab a tub or three for $7 each, except that people in the check-out line will look at you funny if you purchase more than one tub at a time

I am a Red Vine expert. I have a tub of Red Vines on my desk right now. I have 10 empty tubs under my desk. That adds up to 11 tubs of Red Vines consumed by my students since early September. In gross terms (pun intended), this is 44 pounds, 2,750 individual Red Vines, and 73,920 calories in all.

Why my obsession with Red Vines? My theory is that Red Vines are a point of contact. They give students and teachers a chance to be human with each other.

Students must come into my office and ask for a Red Vine. They must say "Please," which they do with varying degrees of hilarious adolescent attitude. They can only take one vine at a time. If they bum rush and take more than one, blaming it on the fact that the vines get stuck together, they get put in the Red Vine penalty box and are banned from Red Vine consumption for 24 hours. Sometimes students come in and "steal" a handful, at which point they must sit through my boring lecture on, "How can you steal that which is freely given?"

They frequently make jokes: "Thanks Mr. Horan, I'll tell my dentist you said hello!" Almost all of them say "Thank you" and mean it. The best thing about Red Vines is the conversations they start. Some would be amazed how much high school students just want to talk, but not their teachers. Red Vines give us an excuse to connect. I have come to believe that Red Vines are like arteries, pumping the life's blood of relationship, turning an anonymous crowd into the beloved community.

A great school is a Red Vine sort of place. One of our school's core beliefs is that *"Healthy and meaningful relationships between students and adults are the foundation for student growth."* Imagine this recipe:

- assemble one core of full grown, attentive, skillful, committed adults;
- mix in 900 creative, hormonal, resistant, uncommitted students;
- create a community where there are a million points of rich human contact;
- and have a Red Vine sort of place.

THIS IS HOW THE AMISH SING

They gather in a big circle organized by gender and voice. There is no leader of song, no cantor, no director. They face each other in a circle and proceed to sing at, with, and for each other. This shift in geometry creates beautiful music. All the parts matter:

- the sopranos can't make it without the basses, etc.,
- the timing, volume, and harmonies feel organic,
- the proximity of the singers is essential,
- music and community emerge, indistinguishable and simultaneous.
- at the center is the song, and the singers themselves are the song.

We teachers must say thanks to each other in the same way the Amish sing. That is, we must shift our Geometry of Thanks to a circle. A great school is the work of a thousand hands. We can't make it without each other. Parents, teachers, volunteers, support staff, thought leaders, board members, administrators, counselors — all are essential, and our timing and harmony must be spot on for all of this to work.

And at the center of our circle are our students. All our pushing, prodding, and planning has conspired to release their voices. Is there anything more beautiful than when their intellect, heart and passion for a better world harmonize?

I have loved being part of our school circle. I have loved the proximity of our voices and how essential we are, one part to the other. And most of all, I loved the center of our circle, our powerful students, our hymn to the world.

YOU THINK OF ME
WHEN I'M NOT THERE?

One of our students, Enrico, came up to me after dismissal one day. He told me that in the space of eight days his cousin and one of his best friends had been killed by gun violence. He had one of those haunted, million-mile-away stares that war vets often exhibit. He told me that his mom was worried about him and asked him to talk to someone. He asked me if I could find him a grief counselor or "something like that." Can you imagine how much Enrico was hurting to actually ask for that kind of help?

I dutifully wrote down a reminder note that I put in the stack of other reminder notes. (I now need reminder notes to help me remember to check my reminder notes.)

Enrico stopped into my office for a Red Vine one day the next week. While handing over a Red Vine and a piece of gum, I told him that I hadn't forgotten his request to find him a grief counselor. I showed him the reminder note. He was amazed. He said, "You think of me when I'm not here?"

Yes, Enrico, I think about you and your fellow students all the time. There it is — the most important reminder. Great teachers believe that all growth: intellectual, emotional, physical moral, spiritual, and developmental happens in the context of deep relationships between searching young people and mindful adults. This is a great school's first and most important lesson plan. Our relationships with our kids must be true blue. We must think of them when they are not here. We must remember who they are and who they can be when they forget themselves.

This is hard, especially during these years of having to do more with less. It is hard to stay true blue when we are tired, swamped, anxious, or frustrated. It is hard to do during the last few weeks of a quarter or a semester when kids are trying to do in three weeks what they should have done during the previous three months.

But there it is, our first priority, our best promise to them: We remain mindful of them at all times. We must stay in deep, robust relationships with the kids with whom we are blessed. We must think of them even when they aren't here.

So have a great week. I'm off to find a grief counselor.

UBUNTU

We teachers often ask the typical questions about how well we did:

- What percentage of our students graduate?
- Do our ACT or other standardized test scores rise every year?
- What percentage of our graduates are accepted by one or more colleges?
- How many make it to their first college class?
- How many graduate from college?
- How many got financial aid or scholarships?
- Whether or not they go to college, do they find fulfilling work?

Such metrics are one way to think about what we did for our students. Another way to size up our teaching, however, is to think about what our kids did for us. *Ubuntu* is a South African idea that states a person is a person only through other people. That is, we come to our own rich, robust humanity only through engaging other humans. *Ubuntu* is as true for teachers and school staffs just as much as it is true for our students.

How do our students enrich our humanity? How do our beautiful, rambunctious adolescents deepen our own personhood? It is one of the great gifts of teaching, this understanding of *ubutu*: we come to be us through our kids.

∞

Here are a few *ubuntus* (is that a word?) that my students have taught me:

- Watching seniors come up to receive their diplomas always deepens our sense of wonder. Who could have predicted four years earlier that so many of our unformed, knuckle-headed freshmen would grow into such interesting young adults?
- After 30 years of working with kids, I am a lot humbler. I find I know next to nothing about how trauma affects my students or how to offer them the best instruction and patient love I have in me.
- I also complain less. (You are welcome to fact check this claim with my wife. On second thought, don't.) On any given day, though, I do realize my biggest challenges are insignificant compared to what our students handle every day.
- I also long more for peace. We have worked so hard at teaching our kids to be peacemakers. Whether they are in the middle of our halls or in a gym after a testosterone-laden first punch has been thrown, our students teach us that peace-making is HARD, GRINDY work.

That may be the most important thing they have taught me, again and again.

- I am funnier, or at least I hope I am. Our kids make me howl with laughter, and I think they like it when I am funny back. Teachers being funny is similar to students learning our first names or some other personal fact about us: It makes us more human, more accessible.

What are some of your *ubuntus?*

SMART PREACHER

I had dinner once with a pastor of a mainline Protestant church. She is a terrific preacher who takes her sermons very seriously. She speaks Greek, so she is able to read the New Testament texts in almost their original forms. She understands the geographical and historical contexts in which those biblical readings are placed. She is a serious theologian and a voracious reader.

And at the end of explaining all the serious preparation that goes into her Sunday homily (two hours for each delivered minute, she claimed), she shared what she considered the most important, most fundamental element in preaching: "Love," she said. "Your congregants have to know and feel that you love them."

Smart preacher.

We teachers are also a seriously prepared bunch. We are degreed, experienced, and prepared. We share high quality professional development and collaborate on lesson plans, student assessments, and Standards Based Grading. We welcome feedback and integrate our peers' best advice.

But the most important, most fundamental element in great teaching is love. Our students must know and feel that we love them. Although our love takes many forms, it is indispensable. This is easy to forget but impossible to do without.

So go get 'em! There will be a student in front of you today who will need the best of your love. Smart preacher = smart teacher.

STAIRWAYS

Stairways are the most optimistic of architectural ideas:

- They are based on the conviction that all rising is incremental.
- They go step-by-step and up-and-down at the same time.
- They stretch our tendons, burn our lungs, and test our will.
- They measure progress in inches.
- They require a constant expense of energy, no matter how depleted or full our batteries may be.
- They are an act of faith in an unknown landing that lies far ahead.

We teachers are also the most optimistic of architects:

- We know all rising is incremental.
- We know learning can go down as well as up.
- We believe students grow step-by-step and that every stair is built on the ones that went before.

- We understand that everything we do, every interaction, admonition, redirection, and affirmation will, inch by inch, lift our students toward the full-grown life they deserve.

Teaching is an act of faith. We may never see the landings and there are no guarantees we will get to the top floor. but on we go. That is beauty enough to get us through the day. See you on the stairs!

THE POWER OF RECOGNITION

She stands barely five feet. All bone and gristle. Silence is her preferred mode of communication. Her hooded eyes say everything that needs to be said.

I met Alisa in public speaking class, not exactly her favorite thing. The first time I even heard her talk was when she asked me to review a draft of a speech about someone who had "left a tattoo" on her heart. She wanted to talk about her cousin, who was more a brother to her. He lived with her family and looked out for her like all great big brothers do. He was a basketball star and never treated her like a girl when they played together. Her game on the court certainly shows that grit.

It broke her heart when her cousin/brother was murdered not far from their home three years before. During her speech, she wore "#3" in his honor. When she spoke, nobody breathed a sound. None of us — teachers, students, staff — had ever heard Alisa speak so clearly and profoundly. From that point on, I called her "#3." She would get mad when I called her by her real name, amazed that I had not comprehended how important my using a nickname was for her. The tattoo on her heart was number shaped. How could I have been so dense?

I drove Alisa to the airport for her first college visit. She was stopped by security. She had no state ID or driver's license. She had brought her high school ID and high school schedule, hoping for a break. The TSA guy called his supervisor, who called his supervisor. Three of them took #3 off to the side while the crowd gaped, eyeballing her every move.

She was bossed around. She was wanded. She was frisked. She was x-rayed. The beleaguered TSA team had no idea they were searching a ticking time bomb. Finally, they let her through. She was fuming, a heartbeat away from saying "F-IT! I'm going home." But she didn't. Her grit and her love for her cousin/brother got her through. Going to college was her way of living the life he did not get to live. When she fumed that she had been treated like a terrorist, I had to amend her nickname. From now on she would be known as "OSAMA bin #3" — our own private joke, our own secret connection.

Schools depend on connections. Those connections happen when we teachers understand our students' tattoos, when we share a nickname or funny memory, when we have gone the extra mile — not out of obligation or job responsibility but out of attentive love. There are plenty of opportunities to love our students. We just have to stop being so dense.

BEST OF MY LOVE

I have always thought that we teachers should give an appreciation dinner for all our significant others. Think about it. When people hear about what we do and where we do it, we usually get all sorts of positive feedback. People understand and appreciate the sacrifice our work entails.

But what about our spouses, our friends, our kids, our parents? Sometimes they might not get the best of our love because we have spent most of it at school that day. We signed up for this mission. Our loved ones did not, but they must still deal with what little there is left of us when we get home.

Our loved ones may worry about our physical safety. They may put up with our anxiety, lethargy, complaining, and school-related obsession. They are the ones who lift us up on difficult Monday mornings and gather up what is left of us on Friday nights.

One teacher told me that when he woke up one morning and was thinking of calling in sick, his wife said, "A sick you is better than no you." How is that for amazing grace? The truth is that we teachers cannot do what we do without the love of our significant others.

My wife, Mary, and I have no children of our own. Therefore, I have no idea how teachers with children go home and give them the attention they deserve when they have been lavishing their love on their students. Talk about a Sophie's Choice! Love is what it takes to teach, but there is not an endless supply of the stuff in our hearts. Or is there?

Here is my suggestion. Make sure that at some point every week you thank your loved ones. Apologize to them for how ground down you sometimes get. Let them know that they are the love of your life, but that sometimes your students are a close second. And then prove to them that you will never, ever take their enervating love for granted.

In addition, I recommend some pasta and a good bottle of red, but I'll leave the specifics up to you.

ACCEPTING GRATITUDE GRACIOUSLY

- "Thanks for everything!"
- "I really appreciate all you have done for my child."
- "Thank you guys, SO much."

Such simple expressions of gratitude, usually texted by students or parents to us, are always tender and usually come out of the blue. They are not perfunctory, or a matter of good manners. They stop us cold. They are time-out-of-time expressions of real gratitude that we teachers will never erase and to which we need to accept and return graciously.

Gratitude is testimony to a certain attentiveness, a simple indication that our kids and their parents know that we have walked the extra mile for them. They speak to us not out of a sense of obligation. They know we act the way we do not because of guilt, pity, or job responsibility. That really — no b.s. — we act out of love. And their simple expression of gratitude is love too.

When our students say thanks, it feels so unplanned, so unrehearsed. They almost surprise themselves by saying it. Maybe they act a bit embarrassed. Their sincerity is unmistakable. Saying "Thanks!" to us deepens them. Receiving their thanks deepens us. We are etched by it. We will wear it for the rest of our lives like a badge of honor.

Gratitude is the sound love makes when it arrives just in time.

PART THREE
WHAT IS
THE COST?

In Love's Service,
Only Wounded Soldiers Can Serve.

Thorton Wilder

- Children break.

- They are abandoned like cheap luggage at a bus station. They are punctured like balloons on the sharp end of fren-emies' jabs. They lose love and settle for less. Their center of gravity is upended by death that comes too soon and too often.

- Adults who should know better, don't. Children carry trauma subdermally, a thin skin satchel waiting to burst. They come unmoored, adrift in a sea of woe. They breathe and move but have no being, having forgotten who they really are.

- Teachers must, perforce, gather. Although we cannot know our students' pain first-hand, we can be present to it. All they ask is that we be proximate, attuned and quiet enough so that they can be heard. We must resist the temptation of a quick fix, an efficient referral or the subtle stiff-arm of generic advice.

- As they unburden their hearts to us, we are broken too. Hearing and holding their pain costs us too. There is no cheap grace, no shortcuts to authentic comfort. It will require the best of our love and draw on limited stores of our energy. We must play the long game because grief takes time.

- This is in the small print of every teachers' covenant with their students. We must be ready to pay the price that love demands. We must contend with their shrapnel. We must honor the courage it takes them to come to us with courage enough to be a sentinel at the fractured doorway of their hearts.

SPENT

I pass three schools in the last blocks of my drive to the school where I teach. As I pass, I pray for the staff in those buildings. I pray for a renewal of their energy, resilience and persistence, especially on Monday mornings when their road to rest is still so long away.

Simultaneously, after 20 years of teaching I realize how little of that energy remains in me. Unlike them, I can no longer give what the week to come will surely require.

I am spent:

- I have taken the better part of myself and spent it.
- I have spent the profligate vigor of a young teacher pulling 14-hour days, heedless of the diminishment that long love requires.
- I have spent my spirit's robust optimism, now tempered by all the assaults on hope, the capricious violence, and the accumulated losses that proximity to poverty demands.

- I have spent my acuity; my attention span now diminished by countless "to do" lists, shifting priorities, schedule-wrecking emergencies, and the non-stop interruptions that make linear thinking so hard to maintain.
- I have spent my old assumptions and my old self.

But I am not unhappy with being spent.

Spent implies treasure given up in return for something of surpassing worth. I have spent willingly, maybe wantonly, in my teaching. To do such important work with people you love for the young people you love is the rarest of joys. It is our students, their potency, their surprising future, their tender gratitude, their desire to repair the world…. This is what my wanton spending has purchased.

I KNOW WHY THE PRINCIPAL SIGHS

The first sigh happens while she and her computer are warming up. It is a long release of breath, a white flag waved in surrender to the over-whelming force of her TO DO list. She bids sad farewell to her weekend's rest, welcoming the clear-eyed knowledge of what her vocation will demand of her this week.

There is no gradual acceleration in schools. Things go from 0 to 150 mph in a heartbeat. Her sigh is the sound every teacher and administrator makes when entering the world of "school as it is":

- Spending time helping students undo the knots of their lives.
- Unraveling crippling consequences from bad decisions made months ago, strand by tangled strand.
- Boosting the confidence, not only of the students and parents but of the teachers and staff.
- Defusing embarrassment,
- Lavishing understanding.
- Recognizing full well that students have the utter freedom to completely wreck their own lives.

- Starting anew the long, fragile path to hope once again.

She sighs, aware how much altitude must be gained before the plane can clear the obstacles and soar yet again.

And then they come, the walking wounded. She is like a confessor listening; her head bowed, her hands clasped, her eyes hollowed out in empathy. In the face of such rare attentiveness, the students sometimes share the untold story they bear: a catalogue of brutal heartbreaks barely admitted to themselves, much less to a friend, much much less than to any adult. Although she cannot completely feel their pain, she can stand in intimate proximity. Such healing presence exacts its own cost, and so she sighs, knowing full well there is no cheap grace.

YOU DO TOO MUCH!

How many times have you seen this happen?

A student balls up his right hand and slams it into his open-palmed left hand, and exclaims something like, "ON MY MOMMA, THIS SCHOOL DO TOO MUCH!"

Love that smack. It is like the whine of an airplane engine fighting off gravity and struggling for flight.

Our students are not the only ones who are struggling for flight. We teachers are dragging too. Our physical, emotional, and spiritual savings accounts are close to overdrawn. The bags under our eyes have bags. Teaching is hard, hard work, and it shows on each of us. We ball up our right hand, slam it into our open-palmed left hand, and exclaim, "ON MY MOMMA, THIS SCHOOL DO TOO MUCH!"

Do our schools DO too much? We certainly hope so, despite:

- Times when a day's instruction feels like a pyrrhic victory.
- Times when the crippling trauma our students carry, carries into us.

- Times when there is too much cruelty, too much bad history, too many odds stacked against our kids.
- Times when we come to feel like lifeguards on the banks of a river of woe.

Schools DOING TOO MUCH isn't new. Teachers have been trying to do too much since Socrates tried to school Plato. We will continue to do so until the last light is turned out. When a school seeks to break the terrible dangers of poverty and ignorance, we teachers should strive to overperform. Gritty, resilient, tactical hope is what will light the way.

But, in the end, it is our kids who will discover their own amazing saving grace, glad that *their* school DID too much.

A "DOOKEY ASS" DAY

I agreed to fly with David on the first leg of his flight to Birmingham, Alabama, because he asked me to. One of those "above and beyond" things teachers sometimes do.

I knew we were in trouble when I saw the 20-inch gash in his duffle bag. He was already 30 minutes late for our 5:00 am Uber pick-up and had slept through my phone calls and texts. An extended doorbell ring finally did the trick. David emerged apologetic and sleepy eyed, his girlfriend stumbling behind him, grasping his arm, reluctant to let him go. When we piled into the Uber, of course, the duffle bag began spilling its contents. Absent a darning needle and canvas patch, he had NO chance of getting the wounded duffle bag on the plane.

Trying to keep the hysteria and frustration out of my voice, I sternly instructed David to grab what was absolutely essential from his duffle bag and stuff it into his bookbag. He left his play station console, three basketball shoes, his sobbing girlfriend, and his distracted father huddled on the curb at Midway Airport.

We barreled through the airport but were stopped by security. David had no drivers' license (having lost it the night before speeding in his girlfriend's un-insured car). His application for a state ID, a copy of the ticket, his high school and college-application ID pictures did not satisfy the TSA security team. He went through the rigorous TSA inspection while precious time ticked away.

We made it to the gate with 7 minutes to spare, only to board the aircraft and sit on the runway for 40 minutes. Which made us late for his connecting flight in Houston to Birmingham. The next flight to Birmingham was at 7:00 pm. It was 11:00 am in Houston.

A lunch of Buffalo Hot Wings ate up 40 minutes. We had another six hours to wait. David napped. He texted and napped some more. He watched basketball videos and napped some more. He called the basketball coach who was recruiting him and arranged a ride to his college at 8:00 pm. He napped some more. He guarded the electric outlet and charger as if his life depended on it. As did mine — waiting in an airport is a killer when you don't have a good book to read.

I finally left David at 5:30 pm, getting the last direct flight back to Chicago. When I arrived, David had called. It was 8:30 pm and his flight to Birmingham was delayed again because of mechanical difficulties. He finally boarded at 10:00 pm. It would be well past midnight before he arrived at his dorm room (picked up by that kind coach who had never met him before) almost 22 hours after his frantic repacking in the speeding Uber.

David called me the next day. He said that yesterday had been one "dookey ass day." Couldn't have said it better myself. But it meant the world to him that we had done it together. We were now sort of a band of brothers, having been knitted together through our shared trials and tribulations.

There are many, many trials and even more tribulations being a teacher. Nothing is easy. Nothing follows a straight path. There will be gob-smacking obstacles so stunning that no one would be able to dream them up. But enduring these things together with our students knits us together, sometimes better than the "dookey ass days."

FUNCTIONAL INDIFFERENCE

It was the only thing she could do: stand as a silent sentry while the indifferent evening rush hour swept by. Janay's bus stop had been commandeered. If an award could be given for assembling the most creative "home" for the homeless, this bus shelter would win hands down. Frank Lloyd Wright could not have done better.

The bus shelter had three plexiglass walls, one of which sported a poster for upcoming performances of the "West Side Story." The irony was unintentional. Covering the open space were two long blue plastic tarps draped over the rickety roof of the shelter and held down by two plastic garbage containers, make-shift Dorian columns courtesy of the Chicago Department of Sanitation.

Inside on the wooden bench lay a pile of ragged clothing, the flotsam and jetsam of a million Salvation Army stores. The pile covered an unmoving human figure of non-descript gender.

Janay was pinioned — caught between the necessity of catching her bus home and the demands of empathy. She knocked repeatedly on the plexiglass wall, even poking her head through the tarps, asking if she could help, unsure of what "helping" even meant. No reply. No movement. No clue.

So Janay stayed, a silent sentry choosing an uneasy presence rather than convenient flight. She offered a bottle of water to the figure, a tangible something rather than nothing. She knew that, on some inchoate level, to leave might get her home sooner but, in the long run, would cripple her activist heart, a price she was unwilling to pay.

Twenty minutes later, the pile moved and a woman emerged. She said not a word, but stuck her hand out for the bottle of water. She and Janay got on the next bus. Separately but together.

Functional indifference to suffering quickly becomes a habit, an all-too-familiar default in a city so fraught with need. We teachers need the example of our young students and their beating activist hearts to remind us where the demands of empathy begin…and to save us from our indifferent rush.

EARLY ONSET

Teachers do not get into teaching to say "NO!"

We are an affirming bunch. Our optics are optimistic: We cannot help but see the "what could be" in each child.

Our preference is to play the long game. We fiddle with the locks on their hearts, believing that each student has a secret combination that we are just a hair's breadth away from discovering. We never give up on a kid, ascribing their lack of response to some fault in our tactical approaches.

We cannot help ourselves. This orientation is a constitutive part of our being, our abiding vision--a deep, archetypal insistence that our skillful, stubborn love can accelerate any student's transformation. We are wired this way. There is no getting around it, we start each day with the commitment to never say "NO."

Until, one day, we do start to say "NO!" It is a gradual diminishment:

- Our steadfast love becomes intermittent.
- Our eyes dim and we see less and less of the dimensions of our students' complicated lives.

- The artery between our heart and our head occludes.
- We leave some stones unturned.
- We do not act on the sudden insight into a student that might make all the difference.
- The "ping" goes unanswered.

We still know what the extra mile requires. It is just that it feels too far to walk. We have not forgotten what is most true about teaching. It is just that we have lost a step. We attended too many feckless faculty meetings. We've had too few classroom wins. We've had too much November or too much March. Too much administrivia. Too much whatever. We begin to forget ourselves. Not completely, not all at once, but some. And that is the pain of it. We know what we are losing. It is early onset of teacher burnout.

Like most important therapy, there are no quick fixes for this: Counsel from wise colleagues. Extra time with the students who too often are on the pay-no-mind list. A mental health day that turns a three-day weekend into a mini-vacation. Prayer. Exercise. Naps.

All of these helps. But mostly, it is the reclamation of our trust—in ourselves, in our colleagues, in our school, in our parents, in our students. This reclamation is part of the winnowing process which makes older teachers great. We begin to trust that we will not forget who we are but come to know real hope more deeply, that what has called us to the great task of teaching will not abandon us now.

RECONFIGURING TOGETHER

Einstein said that no energy in the universe is ever lost. It is just reconfigured. The same can be said of suffering. Suffering never dissipates; it moves on and is reconfigured within the hearts of those most proximate. This is especially true of teachers.

It is no wonder that yesterday at 3:00 pm the teachers on the street side of the building felt they were under siege. It is no wonder that the rest of the faculty, making their ways to their cars that were hemmed in by police tape, felt trapped. It is no wonder that, in helping our kids to see their future, the principal's eyes went dim.

All teachers' heads are on a 180-degree swivel. Our hearts grow weary and our resilience gets ground down. The truth is that we cannot really show love unless we stand in solidarity with our kids and families in their worst moments. We will never know what our kids feel day in and day out. We have only the faintest inkling. But in remaining proximate to their suffering, in being willing to have some of their suffering be reconfigured in us and emerge as a deeper empathy, in making a renewed commitment to help change things, we are doing something really special. Even in the midst of a protest or a pandemic.

Later, while she was ducking under police tape to go home, I asked a teacher if she chose this work or if this work had chosen her. She immediately responded that she chose teaching and will choose it again and again, including the proximity to suffering it sometimes brings. Teaching gives us a chance to reconfigure that which is broken.

I am so glad that we are configuring together.

YOU CAN ALWAYS SEE THE STARS

Keith returned to us with stars in his eyes. It is not an uncommon look for our returning alumni. This college freshman nearly burst with pride as he described his college to some teachers who welcomed him back to our school for a visit.

"It is wide open at my college," he told us. "You can see the stars. You can't always see them in the city."

This good news was right on time for me that day. I struggle with Chicago's unrelenting winter invading my borders. For educators, the problem is especially acute. We are the firelighters, the architects of hope. We help our students bloom in the whirlwind. We are in the service of resilient joy. But there are days when, overwhelmed by fatigue, work, and the sheer costliness of doing great school, we wonder if night is the natural condition of our world.

But our star-gazing grad said, "It is wide open at my college. You can see the stars." Seeing the stars is everyone's best move. No sense denying or insulating ourselves from the night. The night is overwhelming, but the stars steal the show.

We set our compasses, orient our humanity, and find our better angels by star light. We understand that we are from love, by love, and for love at night. We are star-bright, our luminosity made all the more precious by the encroaching night.

We teachers can't always see the stars. Luckily, our students keep us star gazing. They are our saving grace. The constellation of our alumni, students, their families, and our faculty and staff helps us gaze true north.

As the saying goes, "You can only give from that which your purse holds." It is time to fill our purses. Abundant helpings of loved ones, good food, good wine, raucous laughter, and abundant sleep are helpful. Stars are required.

DRIVE-BY-HEART SYNDROME

Every morning and evening I drive to and from work. And every morning and evening I drive past the same five people on the same stretch of sidewalk.

Two sleep side by side on a heating grate, their clothes carefully folded and their haphazard possessions stuffed into milk crates. Two others are usually propped up against the wall. They are all as thin as the collapsed cardboard boxes upon which they sleep. The fifth sits apart from the others, bundled in a red and white blanket, a grey veil over her face, rocking back and forth. She seems to be the furthest gone.

I don't know what is worse. To drive by them every day and not see them, or to drive by, see them and then do nothing. I am in the latter category. I suffer from drive-by-heart syndrome.

Drive-by-heart syndrome is characterized by a numbed sense of moral outrage. It beats faintly through occluded blood vessels. It is long on excuses and short on action. In the face of so many wrongs to right, the drive by heart chooses not to engage at all in most (or sometimes all) of them.

We teachers, however, are saved from drive-by-heart syndrome by our schools. They are our morning's destination and our evening's point of departure. Schools anchor our drive by hearts. They give us a place to take a stand in a morally compromised world. If we "do" school to the best of our ability, there will be a smidgen more justice in the world. Our students' sons and daughters will have a home. Our drive-by-hearts may even find a pulse on our drive home.

THE NEXT RIGHT THING

Monique was the best in the business at setting an appointment with me and cancelling it with plausible explanations, always texted, usually early in the morning when I had come in specially to meet with her. Here were some of her notable excuses:

- My sister had a seizure.
- My grandad fell.
- My mother fainted.
- I am going to have an emergency MRI from these headaches I been having.
- I have to go to see a surgeon about my face.
- My allergies flared up.
- I took too much Benadryl last night and I am too drowsy.
- I have to go to church.
- I have a meeting with my therapist—things are tough for me now.
- I'm not dressed appropriately.

Monique does not stand alone in employing this tactic. But for the sheer number of cancelled appointments, she is my reigning queen. (Apparently, she gives herself credit for doing the responsible thing and making the appointment, but self-protects by begging off for some last-minute, semi-plausible priority that cannot be questioned.)

She employs this bait and switch as a sort of protective force field. I think that moving forward for her is sometimes too much. She does not have enough bandwidth to contemplate life beyond her topsy-turvy home. She can think about moving forward, but when it comes to mustering the escape velocity necessary to push beyond the immobilizing gravity, it just feels like too much.

If I push Monique hard and offer enough alternatives, she is likely to give in. This is not a result of my persistence but rather her desire to really change, which comes on and goes out like a weak Internet signal.

Today she actually came in. She said, "I have some problems with my mother and don't want to talk about it. I promise this is not one of the times I'm just making excuses."

She has talked about her mom in the past: How her mother had snatched the gold necklace she gave Monique as a high school graduation gift years ago and then pawned it off to buy crack. How her mother has stated loudly and repeatedly that she definitely wants Monique out of the house ASAP. She talks about her mother like one expecting the onslaught of severe weather.

So Monique and I will piecemeal it. Take baby steps. Push gently through the flimsy excuses. Make some jokes about her repeated excuses. (Just how many kidney stones does your brother have?) Muster some momentum. Build enough trust to talk about what she does not want to talk about.

And figure out together the next right thing.

AFFIRMATION DESERT

I saw a freshman levitate one time. Marco had just received his progress report, and it was filled with A's and B's. This appeared to be a new experience for him. He presented his grades to a crowd of mindful adults, mostly teachers, who immediately lavished praise upon him. It was then that he levitated.

All the experts say what wise teachers know in their deep heart's core: If you really want students to develop, then you should lavish them with praise. Experts say that the ratio of positive to negative comments should be, at the very worst, four positive affirmations for every negative remark they receive. The positive affirmation should be both truthful and specific (not fake, generic praise like, "Hey, terrific job breathing!")

I think that teachers do a pretty good job at this with our kids, but don't we all need to see more of their parents levitating once in a while? Will they ever get as many "your child did an excellent job" notices as they do "your child messed up again" complaints? I think many of our parents, especially in inner city schools, are in an affirmation desert.

When Parents get a call from school, it is usually bad news:

- Your child is late.
- Your child has detention.
- Your child is failing.
- Your child was in a fight.
- Your child is suspended.

It is a wonder that any parent ever answers a call from us. Some of our parents did not have the best experience when they were in high school. When they receive constant bad news about their child, it is like a generational Ground Hog's Day. They are trekking in the Affirmation Desert.

Many of our parents are put upon from so many sides. We can never fully understand their burdens. Think about how welcome even a bit of good news about their child would be. Think about how we can lift their spirits with truthful, specific, positive affirmation about their kids. Think about how they would levitate.

That might make us levitate as well.

PART FOUR

TEACHERS' PRAYER ALONG THE WAY

I will arise and go now,
for always night and day
I hear lake water lapping
with low sounds by the shore;
while I stand on the roadway,
or on the pavements grey,
I hear it in the deep heart's core.

W.B. Yeats

- The debate about whether teachers in public schools should start the day with a prayer is over. The verdict has already come in. Look no further than the classroom bulletin board to learn the outcome. The prayers are posted there.

- Teachers are serial tapers and pinners. Their classroom bulletin boards are filled with quotes, poems and posters that they cannot do without. These sayings crystalize what they think is most important about teaching. They are daily reminders of the essential, spiritual axioms that switch them from OFF to ON. They are life preservers in times of trial. They critique bad practice. When classroom magic happens, they resonate like a steeple bell rung on Sunday morning.

- Growth on standardized tests tells you something about the effectiveness of a school. So do attendance, staff retention and graduation rates. But to get the real story about the "soul" of a school, check the bulletin boards. There you will find a sounding of the school's "deep heart's core."

POSTINGS ON CLASSROOM AND TEACHER LOUNGE BULLETIN BOARDS SEEN ALONG THE WAY

The Noah Principle:
Predicting rain doesn't count,
building arks does.

If we have no peace
it is because we have forgotten
that we belong to each other.

Mother Theresa

Justice is what love looks like in public.

Cornell West

Our greatest glory is not in never failing
but in rising up every time we fail.

Ralph Waldo Emerson

Live!
And have your blooming
in the noise of the whirlwind.

Gwendolyn Brooks

Humility is the belief that you have something to learn
from absolutely everyone.

Special Education teacher's wall

Justice will only be achieved
when those not injured by crime
feel as indignant as those who are.

Solomon

To educate people is to unfit them to be a slave.

Frederick Douglass

Justice is more than a verdict.

Dean of Students' wall

*Our lives begin to end
the day we become silent
about things that matter.*

Martin Luther King, Jr.

*You can only give
from that which your purse holds.*

Sunni mystic

*To be truly radical
is to make hope possible
rather than despair inevitable.*

Raymond Williams

In the end, we will be examined in love.

John of the Cross

Bonum est diffusivum sui.
Goodness gives itself away.

Thomas Aquinas

Tikkun Olam
Repair the World

The Talmud

To bigotry, no sanction.
To persecution, no assistance!

George Washington

Out of the crooked timber of humanity,
no straight thing was ever made.

Immanuel Kant

So the question is not whether we will be extremists,
but will we be extremists for hate
or will be extremists for love?

Martin Luther King, Jr.

Be kind, for everyone you meet is fighting a hard battle.

Plato

Life is a riddle whose only imperfect solution is Love.

Roger Cohen

Love cheats time because it is passed along,
refracted through the generations;
and it's the reason,
with all its illusions,
that we're here in the first place.

Roger Cohen

The arc of the universe is long,
but it bends towards justice.

Martin Luther King, Jr.

We have all known the long loneliness
and we have learned
that the only solution is love
and that love comes with community.

Dorothy Day

I believe that unarmed truth and unconditional love
will have the final word in reality.
This is why right, temporarily defeated,
is stronger than evil triumphant.

Martin Luther King, Jr.

*The best anti-poverty program around
is a world class education.
In this country the success of our children
cannot depend more on where they are born
than on their potential.*

Barack Obama

*Hope has two beautiful daughters;
their names are Anger and Courage.
Anger at the way things are,
and Courage to see they do not remain as they are.*

Augustine of Hippo

Admit something:
Everyone you see, you say to them,
"Love me."
Of course, you do not do this out loud,
 otherwise someone would call the cops.
Still though, think about this,
this great pull in us to connect.
Why not become the one
who lives with a full moon in each eye
that is always saying,
with that sweet moon language,
what every other eye in this world
is dying to hear?

Hafiz

History says, Don't hope
on this side of the grave.
But then, once in a lifetime
the longed-for tidal wave
of justice can rise up,
and hope and history rhyme.

Seamus Heamey

PART FIVE

A TEACHER'S PRAYER FOR THE MORNING DRIVE

Give us this day,
our daily bread.

Jesus

- I begin as I drive to teach each morning. I pass from the anonymous morning rush hour onto the street that will take me to my vocation.

- I say the prayer out loud. I make it a tangible thing, something in the world that can be measured in decibels, air movement, pitch and tone. My prayer goes from intentionality to corporeality. I do it daily. Same time, same place, habitual; this prayer is hard-wired into my muscle memory. Incarnated.

- This same prayer is my audible aspiration, the hoped-for context from which will flow all my day's efforts. Part promise, part reminder, part self-critique. It keeps me driving. And it drives me through the day.

THE FIRST WORD

I take my time with the first word…"**Our.**"

At the corner by the school, they come — "**Our**" students: Huddled, ragged, stiff-legged, resigned, scared, world-weary, but also hopeful, eager, inquisitive, naïve, worldly-wise.

"**Our**" is the trickiest of all personal pronouns. The first word out of our morning prayer for teachers claims that we are utterly, unalterably connected — me in my car with the bent and weary on the other side of the windshield. My students and co-workers at school with all the drivers in all the cars in all the world's morning rush hours. **OUR.** Saying it out loud makes it a promise.

THE SECOND WORD

But this personal pronoun "our" needs a landing place. Our what? Or our who? We are connected to be sure, but by what? Affiliations abound.

Abba/Immah (Papa/Momma). What a landing! It is our petition, our longed-for plea, our outrageous, barely appropriated wish. "We, ours, us." We will say these versions of the same pronoun seven more times in this prayer. There is no missing the intention here. We belong to one another because we have the same parentage. There is no other way.

Now I say it, **Abba/Immah. Papa/Momma.** Not only are we connected, we are siblings! This changes everything. I am three minutes from school and everyone I will see is family, bound by a common parentage.

Abba/Papa. Immah/Momma. A repeated syllable gurgled by an infant swathed in a parent's love. The point is not gender, but intimate dependency. I do not have to be good to be so loved. I must know that I am so loved *in order* to be good. How else can I give what my students and fellow teachers so deeply need?

This does not come naturally to me. It is not my abiding consciousness. I come to **Papa/Momma** on a desperate path. Through long periods of enduring the midnight dogs of depression and anxiety, my **Papa/Momma** is not a noun. It is a plea. I am an infant howling for milk, a child screaming to be held. I utterly depend on **Abba/Immah** on many mornings when I have nothing left.

I come to the sprawling need of school with empty pockets. Left to my own devices, I would turn around, go home, and flick off my light.

And, remarkably so, in such a state of absolute need, I am actually closer to our shared human heritage. We teachers are completely dependent on **Papa/Momma** to make it through the demanding day. Our need for **Abba/Immah** is pure, free from nuance — it is a cry for survival, a longed-for love that we cannot do without. It makes siblings of us all.

WHO ARE IN HEAVEN,
HALLOWED BE YOUR NAME.

"Who, heaven, hallowed." I love speaking out loud these triple aspirations. In winter, I puff out three clouds. Three quick pointed reminders that we are working with a net during this perilous high wire act. Our Papa/Momma is both immanent and transcendent, as present in an alley as in a nebula. The always and everywhere love that beckons our hearts also sets the **heavens** in motion.

YOUR KINGDOM COME,
YOUR WILL BE DONE,
ON EARTH AS IT IS IN HEAVEN.

It so happens that as I speak this, my favorite part of the prayer, I pass a peeling mural on the side of an abandoned building. Rae-Rae was six when he was killed. He smiles into the empty lot next door, the stuffed animals, spent candles, empty Courvoisier bottles long since gone.

"Gone too soon" the mural says. Three or four more windy Chicago winters and Rae-Rae's mural will be as gone as he is. This is old news. When I pray this part out loud, Rae-Rae and me see I-to-I. This is where **the kingdom comes**.

I have two much beloved friends who lost their son Billy in a heartbeat on a soft summer night because human heads are eggshell soft. The only way Billy's mom can navigate her ocean of grief is by bringing heaven and earth together in acts of love. She is closest to Billy when she acts out of and lives within the realm of God's love. When she loves here, when she lives **God's will here**, the distance from her heart to Billy's is membrane thin. They are in the same realm.

I have no idea what will be requested of my heart today. All I have is this prayer on this patch of earth that commits me to bring **heaven and earth together** in acts of love.

GIVE US THIS DAY OUR DAILY BREAD.

The best way I can marry my heart to God's will is to eat my **daily bread**. What happened yesterday? What encounters remain in my heart as yesterday fades from view? A student's exhausted face, a teacher's passionate advocacy, the impulse to call a long-forgotten colleague, the need to apologize to a student who was the target of an anger that she did not cause. **This is daily bread.**

Consciousness of intentionality for me is the yeast. It rises in my soul like baking bread. Eating yesterday's **daily bread** makes me hungrier for this day's spiritual nourishment. The only way I can abide in the realm of love is to eat with others. Working for the kingdom is hard work. We hunger. Abba/Immah's love and will for **us** is taken, eaten, and incarnated. The bakery is always open. We become what we eat.

FORGIVE US OUR SINS AS WE FORGIVE THOSE WHO SIN AGAINST US.

There is no question about it. This is a sneaky proposition.

Do I really want to ask out loud that I be **forgiven my sins** to the same extent that I **forgive the sins of others?** I think of all the grievances I have caged up. I feed them like spoiled pets until they are swollen and sullen. Schools can be such feeding grounds for real and imagined sins. My bandwidth for love is thus compromised by my habit of taking and nurturing offense.

I once asked a wise and holy man about what we experience on the dawn side of our last breath. "Mercy." he said. "Mercy. **We are all forgiven.**" And I know this. When I understand everything important about a student's life, when I take the time to behold each of them, my natural inclination is to have mercy, to increase my bandwidth for love. And they are freed to share with me the untold story they have borne in solitary silence until then.

Mercy. This makes all the difference. **Forgive us our sins AS we forgive others their sins?** We teachers should take that wager. May we be conscious that we are so loved by Poppa/Momma that we practice mercy for all those who come our way today.

DO NOT LEAD US INTO TEMPTATION.

I pause before entering a viaduct. There is a STOP sign. This stretch always gives me pause. The embankment is maniacally overgrown and heavily weeded. Plastic bags caught on stunted trees wave like flags of surrender.

I enter the underpass, a rusty, deteriorating, dank and dirty place where all is shadow and menace. Empty liquor bottles, crushed beer cans, and spent needles, the detritus of despair cover the buckled sidewalk. The street is pot-holed with open asphalt decubiti, the product of long-years of neglect.

This is the place of corrosion. This is the place where all wrong turns converge. Abba/Immah can see all the pain and overwhelming inertia that is to come as consequence of the perfectly wrong choices we will make and watches in horror as we enter the underpass and come undone in slow motion.

Papa/Momma will **not lead us into temptation**, through our self-imposed wreckage. Love will lead us teachers no matter how densely unaware we are. We are not created for the underpass. Abba/Immah will lead us out.

BUT DELIVER US FROM EVIL.

There are days when the race between grace and evil is often a photo-finish. Can there be any doubt that we teachers know this in our heart of hearts? I am sobered by this ending of our prayer. It truly makes me feel that my co-workers, students, and families are knit not only by familial love but by our proximity/vulnerability to evil. I pray these words the loudest, because we who teach are first responders.

We teachers know evil. We know that living a life of virtue is no guarantee against sudden, haphazard, epic tragedy. We know that evil is baked into institutions, habituated and historical. We know that the innocent suffer, that indifference reigns, and that prophets are stoned. We know that some have made a permanent place within their hearts for the great lie, and that they sow destruction and death as they go.

Our out-loud morning prayer does not have a care-free ending. This last **deliver us** is an acknowledgement that marrying our hearts to Abba/Immah's means we will sometimes have to drink from a bitter cup. But we will not do this alone. We have one another.

And we have our teacher's prayer. This will **deliver us from evil** this day.

AMEN.

Yes, it is so!

ACKNOWLEDGMENTS

Mrs. CANT-lin and all the teachers who taught me I could.

Jack Shea who taught me how to see the simple stories and the profound truths they carry.

The students, parents, teachers, and staff of North Lawndale College Prep, who taught me the meaning of *ubunto* — that a person is only a person through other people.

My wife Mary, whose love is my first, best, and only lesson plan.

ALSO AVAILABLE

LITERARY PORTALS TO PRAYER
Excerpts from Classic Literature
Illuminated by passages from
The Message: Catholic/Ecumenical Edition

Louisa May Alcott
Hans Christian Andersen
Jane Austen
Elizabeth Barrett Browning
Charles Dickens
George Eliot
Elizabeth Gaskell
Herman Melville
William Shakespeare
Edith Wharton
Walt Whitman

ACTA PUBLICATIONS
800-397-2282 • www.actapublications.com

ACTA GIFT BOOKS

WHERE GOD IS AT HOME
Poems of God's Word and World
Irene Zimmerman, OSF

INSPIRED CAREGIVING
Weekly Morale Builders
Mary K. Doyle

LEAPS OF FAITH
Playful Poems and Fanciful Photos
Marva J. Hoeckelman, OSB

AN A-Z GUIDE TO LETTING GO
Helen Reichert Lambin

HOW TO AVOID BURNOUT
Achieving Life-Giving Work and Ministry
Carroll Juliano and Loughlan Sofield

ACTA PUBLICATIONS
800-397-2282 • www.actapublications.com